FLYING WORDS

WORDS THAT SPEAK

TANISHKA GARG

Made with ♥ on the Notion Press Platform
www.notionpress.com

To my mother, Dr.Priyanka Garg, and my father, Mr.Rajkumar Garg,

who are always by my side.

To myself,

who is there with me till the end.

Contents

Contents

Foreword

The book includes heart-touching emotions, tears, smiles, and lots of inspiration.

It pushes you to dive deep into the world and makes you think about every written letter.

Preface

Poems aren't only words for me but are friends, who never are away from my heart.

I hail from India. I love interacting with others through poems. My poems are mostly based on human emotions. Apart from writing, I also enjoy reading and dancing.

Acknowledgements

Thanks to everyone who gave me all experiences, which helped me get ideas.

We all have some people who help us change our life, and guide us to the right path, therefore, I would also like to give my gratitude to my family and my teachers.

1. A mask in love

They had a heart of joker,
and they were playing with each other.
The only thing they did was to sit tight and say good-byes to each other.
How would they know they had fellen in love,
when they wore a mask of fear.
They only thing they had in common was a fake smile and tears.
Their eyes showed love,
but they wore dark black shades,
but the atmosphere however told,
how hate was fake.
Now they found the true colors of the love life they wanted to find,
however, they knew their faces were not defined.

2. A little longer

I wish,
I could tell you,
wait a little longer,
to stay beside me,
a little longer.
I wish,
I could say,
how I wanted to extend the memories,
tie new bonds,
and revive the old ones.
I wish,
I could tell,
how I missed singing poems for you,
dancing in the rain,
and seeing fireworks with you.
Sinking into your deep eyes,
staring at your smile,
I wish I could tell you,
how I missed the old times.
I miss your laugh,
I miss the good days,
believe me, admirer,

I miss your written fine lines.
I wish,
I could tell you,
wait a little longer,
to stay beside me,
a little longer.
In this universe I believe,
I could find you again,
with the same scares,
you got while fighting for me that day.
I look up and see millions of stars,
but the moon is you for sure.
I wish,
I could tell you,
wait a little longer,
to stay beside me,
a little longer.

3. Broken Mirrior

I saw that reflection staring at me,
from that broken mirror.
I felt a thousand lies piercing my skin,
through that broken mirror.
All those words echoed in my ear,
spoke the broken mirror.
The truth left me alone,
with the broken mirror.
'I am sorry' I said,
'I am with you' told the broken mirror.

4. Shadow

You have been following me since the day I was born,
you were beside me, even if I was lost.
You never hurt me, never betrayed me,
stood with me even if I was wrong.
You left your fellow brothers,
and made me strong.
You did not change the colors and showed them true,
dear shadow I always want to be with you.

5. Alone for the Walk

Alone for the walk,
went the moon,
to shimmer and glow,
to make it bloom.
Alone for the walk,
went for the moon,
they got jealous of the beauty,
no one possesses.
Moon stands alone between many stars.
Sleep during the day,
wake at the late hours.
Laughs with no one,
have no one to cry with,
but stands there a lot of people dependent on him.
Alone for the walk,
went the moon,
to shimmer and glow,
to make it bloom.
Alone for the walk,
went for the moon,
they got jealous of the beauty,
no one possesses.

6. Normal

Be normal,
I heard,
It is normal for me,
being different,
is best for me.
Socialize,
I heard,
It is social for me,
being alone,
is best for me.
Realize,
I heard,
I realized everything for me,
being close to the truth,
is the best for me.
Move on,
I heard,
I tried for me,
living with the memories,
is the best for me.
Be normal,
I heard,

It is normal for me,
being different,
is best for me.

7. That smile

And what happened to that smile,
I thought it was just gone for a while.
You made me believe it,
and I wasn't able to see the pain.
Ha! How did you even make it possible?
I thought you were unstoppable.
You did not even show a tear,
I thought you will be jolly forever.
And what happened to that smile,
I thought it was just gone for a while.
What happened to, that smile?

8. Just lies

How trustworthy they thought I was,
when they looked into my eyes,
it was just a lie sweetheart,
they were just lies.
How happy they thought I was,
when they looked at my smile,
it was just a lie sweetheart,
they were just lies.
How soft they thought I was,
when they looked at my hands,
it was just a lie sweetheart,
they were just lies.
How miserable they thought I was,
why they heard all the lies,
well..... they were just lies sweetheart,
just few true lies.

9. That hope-My dream

And that hope will never die,
one day my dream will come to life.
I will stand facing all my fears,
laugh at my own tears.
Life,
it will move on,
will make me struggle,
but I will stand strong.
The mirror may get scattered,
but I will try to,
fix it better.
And that hope will never die,
one day my dream will come to life.

10. Painful game

When you meet her,
tell her she was my first family,
put hands on her shoulder and tell her,
my days went out missing her.
Remind her how I was beside her and expected the same,
explain to her how she wasn't greedy nor I was lost in fame.

Bring her to me,
because I want to tell her that we don't have pictures but memories,
which are now nothing but moments,
I want to tell her now nothing but a painful game.

11. The blue gown

He smiled and looked towards me,
he said,
he wanted me to be his queen.
I think he meant it,
because he gave me a golden crown,
I wore a blue gown,
and laughed aloud.
I had a smile crept on my face,
and told him that I wasn't part of his race.

12. Way back down

Looking up the sky,
I realized that it was too high,
I turn around,
round and round,
to find a way back down.
Way back down,
to where I started,
to where it all begin.
Way back down,
to where I lived,
to where I stayed.
Way back down,
to where I suffered
to where there was only pain.
Way back down,
where there was no hope,
and only a death game.
Way back down,
to painful life,
and hurtful days.
Looking up the sky,
I realized that it was too high,

I turn around,
round and round,
to find a way back down.
Way back down,
to where I started,
to where it all begin.
Way back down,
only to find out,
sky was never too high,
for those who want to fly.

13. Alone

I am not lonely,
it's just,
I am standing alone.
In the dark forest,
where anyone barely goes,
on the road,
which no one has thought of.
I am fighting alone,
with a sword and crowd,
which hardly opens up their mouth.
I am facing it alone,
the dark cloud,
searching for the crown,
which none found.
I am alone,
but far there,
someone hopes.

14. Lost

I am lost,
lost in your eyes,
lost in your smile,
lost in fame,
lost in the blame game.
I am lost,
lost in the words,
lost on the road,
lost in the drive,
lost in the destiny yet to arrive.

I am lost,
lost in the deep sea,
lost in the green field,
lost with my dreams,
lost in between the trees.
I am lost,
lost in the chapter,
lost in the book of life,
lost in the page,
lost between the phrases.
I am lost,

lost to be never found,
lost te be heard around,
lost-I am lost.

15. With the pen

With the pen,
we wrote the history,
with the pen,
we write the future.
With the pen,
we wrote the love story,
with the pen,
we write the inventory.
With the pen,
we wrote the glory,
with the pen,
we write the quarry.
With the pen,
we wrote our lives,
with the pen,
we write our cries.
With the pen,
we will change the world,
with the pen,
we will decide our luck.

16. The legend untold

With the flip of pages,
the story reveals,
the legends untold,
aren't any more mysteries.
With the spilled ink,
the hidden truth speaks,
the legends untold,
aren't any more mysteries.
With the toren corners,
the tragedies scream,
the legends untold,
aren't any more mysteries.

17. It's war-full of cries

With the blood-shed skin,
or the tear-shed eyes,
it's war,
full of cries.
With the black smoke,
or dirty clothes,
it's war,
full of cries.
With lost hope,
or dead families,
it's war,
full of cries.
Why are we so ruthless,
why are we so careless,
let's smile,
let us end the war,
full of cries.

18. Memories

Future into present into past,
dreams come true,
but I highly doubt that they last.
Time flies by days past,
how unknown came close,
how friends were left at last.
How they became unknown and part of great moments,
how they became part of every bad comment.
Moments passed by,
the nights fade by,
and finally,
it all becomes memories,

19. Shatered mirror

She may laugh and let it go,
but how sensitive she is inside.
She may smile and stay strong,
but how broken she is inside.
She may be active all day long,
but how she slept crying.
She may say she is fine,
but how well she is at lying.
She may to you and smile,
please let it be for a while.
Who knows,
her heart is nothing,
but a shattered mirror.

20. Live a Long Life

Let us erase all memories,
and take a deep breath,
let us understand,
and make our mind-set,
let us take a few steps,
and go ahead,
let us look up,
and see the world,
let us close our eyes,
and make new ties,
let us sit next,
and be someone's sunshine.
let us not look at time,
and go for a drive,
let us look at sky,
and fly high,
let us walk,
and have a great talk,
let us see,
the moon bright,
let us count,
count the stars,

let us stand,

and lead,

let us fight,

till the last beat,

let us live,

live a long life

21. Hustle up

Aren't you tired of getting jealous,
it's okay if you are below line and average,
Hustle up!
Mold yourself as clay,
be allergic to quitting,
and focus on fair play.
Yeah!
Burn up like fire,
you got it right,
you know,
how to ride,
Bring it up!
show how to deal.
Tell them the consequences to mess with you,
let us work hard and see victory.

22. Me and my dance

I dance to live,
I dance to feel,
I dance to celebrate,
I dance to be me.
My moves represent me,
my heart teaches me.
My legs move in a direction,
my hands flow in a motion,
where it's me.
I jump,
I swing,
I wave,
I tap,
and touch the ground with my sweaty hands.
Dance is a bag full of bags to me,
and is an ocean so blue to me.
I jump in the world of dance with no walls bounding me.
I roe the boat in the river with the waves flowing with me.
With feeling,
with emotions,
with musical beat,
I can jump high,

and began on feet.
With a swirl,
with a tap,
with wind breeze.
I go right,
I go left ,
and mocve ahead.
And with a round,
I am back.
I dance for laughter,
I dance for tears,
I dance for madness,
I dance for fear,
I dance for hopes,
I dance for screams,
I am a dancer,
I creat dreams.

23. If I was a tree

If I was a tree,
I would live in a garden,
full of flowers,
with no pollution.
If I was a tree,
I would go up the hill,
dancing in the forest,
waving with the wind,
chirping with the birds,
swimming in the river,
jumping up and down,
without a reason.
If I was a tree,
I would sleep in a cave,
sit on a chair,
and look at river waves,
eat in a restaurant,
designed by human beings.
If I was a tree,
I would do whatevere I want to,
but not stand in a place.

24. Found

This version of me,
wasn't built in overnight,
this is experience,
this is pain,
this is insecurities,
this is abuse,
this is depression.
I had to go through things to get to the level I am at now.
I am still learning how to go back and reread my own chapters
without feeling like burning those pages.
Sometimes I feel like I want to disappear,
but you really want to be is,
found.

25. Freedom

Today,
I am sitting in front of a wall and writing,
today,
I am facing a big change and fighting.
Yesterday,
the tree was green,
with glossy flowers,
yesterday,
the sly was black,
with lots of stars.
Tomorrow,
will be a huge mountain,
with lots of shrubs,
tomorrow,
will be a blue sky,
with dust.
But a day will come,
when I will water the plants,
the will blossom up,
with loads of flowers.
Then,
I will look up to the sky,

it would be blue and clear again.
A day will again come,
when I will sit in frount of a tree,
and write a poem.
I would learn to drive a car,
but not walk home.
For the freedom I did hope,
for a long time ago.

26. Sleep

I am tired,
I want to sleep,
loneliness is just killing me.
Yes,
I am being mean,
the passion is building me.
The fire,
is burning me,
the tears,
are hurting me.
The pen in my hand is breaking,
the stone kept on my heart is craking.
I am tired,
I want to sleep.

27. Little stones

How happy are the little stones,
rolling on the road alone.
Unbothered by the weather conditions,
singing and dancing in every season,
laughing at every situation,
forgiving the person,
who kicked them earlier.
How happy are the little stones,
rolling on the road alone.

28. Reflection

The scariest thing I have ever faced,
was not a monster,
not even an ugly face.
I was a reflection,
that I saw in the mirror.
All the dark parts were now visible to me,
it was past which was scaring me.
It blocked my future,
but I am still alive,
it is tough,
but it is a fight.
The reflection is scaring me,
is hurting me,
is depressing me,
yet,
it's curing me,
healing me.

29. They told me

Someone close to me,
told me,
that I became rude.
Someone close to me.
told me,
I lost my kindness.
Someone close to me,
told me,
I became negative.
Someone close to me,
told me,
I am not the one they met before.
Yes,
I might become rude,
because I have been ignoring you a bit,
yes,
I might have lost my kindness,
as I am understanding the world in bits.
Yes,
I agree that I might have been negative,
maybe because I lost all my positivity.
I agree I may not be the one you met before,

as in the past,

it wasn't me.

However,

in this world,

I met someone,

who asks me,

"do you know what happened today?"

I met someone,

who told me,

"I won't let you suffer the same"

30. The Sun rise

From a hut,
I was seeing an orange ball,
coming out from its palace,
and bringing a sense of sight to the world.
The giant gaseous ball slowly came up,
completely led by the birds,
snow melting,
and people waking,
the tint of orange,
yellow,
and red,
made me realize the new start.
My hut,
which was on the top of a hill,
glowed up with the flowers opening again.

31. I will smile

No matter what,
I will smile,
even if I don't want to,
I will smile,
even if it's fake,
I will smile.
I will smile,
no matter what,
I will smile,
whatever the conditions be,
I will smile,
even if the scar is deep.
I will look down,
I will smile,
I will go down,
I will smile,
I will face you,
I will smile.
No matter what,
I will keep on the mask of fake smile.

32. New start

You made me write a new start,
so I can rewrite my end,
let's make a new world with no problematic bends.
Yes,
I agree,
it's difficult,
but,
let's come to the fact,
that it's not impossible.
It's hard,
but my dear,
let's solve it together.

33. Them

How careless are they,
breaking the hearts for which they didn't pay.
How mean are they,
thinking for themselves,
even though they sit with each other,
everyday.
Hoe judgemental are they,
judging the smile,
which came after suffering a long way.
How they forgot,
they lived for each other,
unbothered by the world,
smiling seeing each other,
like an idiot.
How could they think they lost each other,
how could they not remember the happy moments they had together.

"Words are something you can't say much about, but they say very much about you"

Printed by Libri Plureos GmbH in Hamburg, Germany